The Land
We Live On

By Carroll Lane Fenton
and Mildred Adams Fenton

GIANTS OF GEOLOGY

IN PREHISTORIC SEAS

OUR CHANGING WEATHER

PREHISTORIC ZOO

ROCKS AND THEIR STORIES

THE LAND WE LIVE ON

To Margo and Fred:
You have asked us what the land is like and how it changes, as well as what happens when people live upon it and use it. Your questions helped us decide what to write about, and you chose some of the pictures that tell the land's story.
Now that the book is published, we are sure you will want to share it with other boys and girls. It will tell them about hills, valleys, and prairies where you live, just as it tells you about land that is dry or high or much more level than the country near your homes.

The Land
We Live On

REVISED EDITION

Carroll Lane Fenton and
Mildred Adams Fenton

DOUBLEDAY & COMPANY, INC.
GARDEN CITY, NEW YORK

ISBN: 0-385-00570-9 TRADE
0-385-04214-0 PREBOUND
Library of Congress Catalog Card Number 66–14864
9 8 7 6 5 4 3

CONTENTS

Land

We see land all around us every day,
so let's find out what it is
and why it is important.
Land is the dry, solid part of our earth—
the part that is not covered with water.
Some land, we know, is made of hard stone
that goes deep, deep down into the ground.
Some land is made of loose sand or soil,
or the kind of soft rock called clay.
Some land is a mixture of different things.
It is a mixture of stones and sand, or of clay and soil,
or of soil and big hard rocks
like those you see in this hilly pasture.

This land is made of
sandy soil and many big,
hard rocks.

8

The land is very important to us
because we and other people live on it.
Many things besides people live on land, too.
It makes homes for plants of different kinds—
for flowers and grass, for weeds and tall trees,
and for all the useful plants that grow
on farms, on ranches, and in gardens.
The land also makes homes for animals
from tiny worms and insects to cattle and horses
that also live on ranches and farms.
Can you think of anything more important
than the solid, dry part of our earth
on which plants, people, and many other creatures
find food and good homes?

Grass, trees, animals,
and many other creatures
live on the dry,
solid land.

Land and Water

The land is so big we sometimes think
that it must be everywhere.
Really, land is only a small part of the earth,
for all the rest is covered with water.
Some water is found in ponds and lakes
where we swim or go boating on summer days.
Water also is found in creeks and in rivers
that flow for miles and miles.
But most water is in the seas and oceans.
Oceans are larger than ponds, lakes, and rivers—
even larger than the biggest lands.
Here is a shore, where land and ocean come together.
We can see only the edge of the ocean.
It goes far beyond the woods, rocks, and sandy beach
that lie at the edge of the land.

At the edge of the
land lie seas and oceans,
where the earth is
covered with water.

Across Our Country

Land is the solid part of the earth,
but it is not the same everywhere.
If we take trips in cars or trains or airplanes
we'll see places where the land is high
and places where it is low.
We shall find rough, hilly land and land that is flat.
We shall visit places where the land gets lots of rain
and shall go to others that are dry
almost every day in the year.
If we like, we can mark each place on a map.
It will show the different kinds of land
that are found in the different parts
of our big, broad country.

This map shows different kinds of land to be seen when we travel across our country.

The Great Plains

Plains are level-looking land where we see
barns, houses, and towns that are far, far away.
Most plains that are near sea coasts are low,
but plains that are far from the sea may be high.
High plains in the West are called the Great Plains
because they are very large.
Some parts of the Great Plains really are level,
but others have ridges, hills, and valleys.
The Great Plains do not get much rain in summer,
when the sun shines brightly
and the wind blows almost every day.
The Great Plains become hot and very dry
when the sun shines and the wind keeps on blowing
day after day after day.

This part of the
Great Plains looks level,
or almost flat.

Prairies

The word "prairie" means a grassy place among trees.
But big prairies in the central part of our country
have thousands and thousands of grassy places,
and thousands of groves of trees.
Prairies are not so flat as most plains,
and they are not so dry and windy.
They have hills and low, rounded ridges;
they have creeks that run past the hills,
and rivers that flow toward the ocean,
which is miles and miles and miles away.
Prairies also have farms with fields of grain—
with white houses and sheds, and big red barns,
and cattle that feed in grassy pastures.
It is fun to watch cattle and count the barns
while we ride across the prairies.

Prairies have grassy places
and trees and many,
many farms.

Deserts

Deserts are found in the western part of our country,
between long mountain ranges.
Many deserts are sandy or dusty, and are dry
because they do not get much rain.
When rain does fall, most of the water runs away.
It runs away in rivers and in creeks
that flow through narrow, steep-sided valleys
or spread out and make ponds on low, flat places.
When the rain stops
all these creeks and rivers dry up,
and so do the ponds in low places, or basins.
Soon the deserts have no more water
than they had before the rain.

Many deserts are
sandy and are dry
because they do not get
much rain.

Some deserts do not have trees,
for trees cannot grow on very dry, sandy land.
Other deserts have almost no plants at all
because the ground is full of salt and other things
that keep plants from growing.
But most deserts are not so dry or so bare.
They have a few small trees that live in low places
where water stays deep down in the ground.
Deserts also have bushes that grow in green domes,
as well as cactus plants that spread out on the ground
or stand up straight, like green tree trunks
that have spines instead of leaves.
Such plants are able to live in the desert
because they do not need much water
and can stand the hot, dry summer days.

Some deserts are
stony land where small
bushes and spiny
cactus plants grow.

Hills and Valleys

There are hills in many parts of our country—
even on prairies, deserts, and plains.
Hills are places where the land is high and rough,
with ridges and steep slopes.
Roads often wind in and out around the ridges
or climb their sloping sides.
Creeks and rivers wind in and out, too,
but they never wind their way up slopes.
Instead, they flow through low places called valleys
that lie between the hills.
This river is flowing through a valley
between hills that are covered with trees.

These hills are higher
than the valley through
which a small river flows.

24

Buttes

Many hills are close to other hills,
just as people stand close to each other
when they are in a crowd.
But hills on the Great Plains are not crowded,
and many of them stand out alone.
These lone hills on the plains are often called buttes.
So are other steep hills that stand alone
in the middle of big, flat-bottomed valleys.
"Butte" (byoot) is a French word for "steep hill."
It was used long, long ago by men
who came from the French part of Canada.
These men climbed buttes to look across wide valleys.
They watched for lone hills that showed them where to go
when they traveled across the plains.

Here is one of the
steep hills, or buttes,
that stand upon the
Great Plains.

26

Mesas
and
Tablelands

The word "mesa" (MAY-sah) is Spanish. It means "table,"
and mesas are table-shaped hills in the West.
They have steep, bare-looking sides and level tops
that are made of strong, hard stone.
A few mesas stand alone, like buttes,
in the middle of wide, grassy plains.
But most mesas are found on dry deserts,
or in valleys among mountains and high, level places
that are known as tablelands, or plateaus.
When you see one of these tablelands in the West
you may think that it looks like a big mesa
with steep, bare sides and a level top
that is covered with strong, hard stone.

Mesas are table-shaped
hills with flat tops
that are made of strong,
hard stone.

Badlands

Badlands in the West got their name
because they were bad, or difficult, country to cross
in the days when there were no roads.
Most badlands look almost like deserts
with many valleys and steep, bare hills
that are made of clay or shale and sandstone.
Some valleys are wide and others are narrow.
Some hills are long, sharp ridges,
but others are small mesas or buttes.
When the sun shines, the badlands become hot and dry.
But when rain falls, water runs down the hillsides
and covers the bare bottoms of valleys
with soft, sticky mud.

Badlands like these
have bare hills and ridges
made of clay or soft
sandstone.

Lava Plains

Many dark-colored, stony plains in the West
were made when melted rock called lava (LAH-vah)
came out of big cracks in the ground.
At first the lava was hot and soft, or runny.
It was so soft that it spread out over flat places.
It was so runny that it flowed into valleys
until they were full.
While the lava was spreading and flowing, it cooled
and turned into hard, dark stone.
Where the stone was piled up high, it made buttes.
It also hardened in ridges and mounds and queer twists
that formed where the lava rolled over and over
before it cooled and became stone.

This dark lava
came out of the ground
while it was hot and
soft, or runny.

Mountains

Some mountains look like low, rounded hills
that have grassy slopes and groves of trees
all the way to their tops.
Many people live among low mountains.
Some people live in towns or on ranches and farms
where they raise cattle or grow sugar beets and corn.
Farmers who live among other low mountains grow fruit.
They grow grapes and peaches, prunes and apples
which are sold to people who live in cities
where there isn't enough room to grow things.
When you ride among low mountains like these
look for farms with fields and ranches with pastures.
Look for orchards and vineyards in the valleys
and on sloping mountain sides.

People grow crops
of fruit among these low
mountains.

Other mountains are steep and very high.
They have rocky slopes and cliffs like stone walls.
They have ridges and pointed tops, or peaks,
that are partly covered with snow and ice.
The valleys between these high mountains are narrow
and some of them are very deep.
Many mountain valleys contain lakes
that are filled with water from melting snowbanks
or with rain water that runs into the valleys
from ridges and peaks and cliffs.
In summer people come to these high, snowy mountains.
The people come to hike and ride and climb the peaks,
or to camp and fish and have good times
beside the deep, cool lakes.

These mountains are
steep and rocky.
They are partly covered
with ice and snow.

Crumbling Rocks

The land is big and strong and solid,
yet things change it every day.
Some changes begin when rain falls or snow melts
and the water soaks into rocky ground.
Water does things to solid bits, or grains, in the rocks.
It makes some grains grow larger and larger.
It makes other grains so soft
that they let beds or ledges of stone
crumble into pebbles and sand.
When the pebbles and sand roll down steep banks
they leave blocks and rounded lumps of stone
that have just begun to crumble.

Water is making this rock
crumble into pebbles and
grains of sand.

Clouds and Rain

Other changes in the land begin
when storm clouds roll across the sky
and raindrops patter down.
"Pat-pat-spat!" go millions of raindrops
as they come out of the storm clouds
and fall upon the land.
Some drops fall on trees or on grassy places
where they stay and slowly soak into the ground.
Other raindrops fall on ground that is bare.
These drops soon make the bare ground wet
and turn its surface into mud.
Muddy splashes pop up into the air
when raindrops patter down very hard
upon the bare, wet ground.

These storm clouds make
millions of raindrops
that fall to the ground.

Rill Marks

"Pat-pat! Patter-spat!" Raindrops keep on falling.
Soon they fall too fast to soak into the ground.
They begin to run away over the surface
in tiny, muddy streams called rills.
Rills are muddy because they are full of soil grains.
They get the soil bit by bit,
pulling and tugging at every grain
until it comes loose from the ground
and is whirled away in the water.
Soon the water takes so much soil away
that it makes little ditches, or rill marks.
Here are some rill marks that were made
by water that washed soil grains away
when rain fell very hard.

Rain water that washed
soil grains away
made these rill marks
in a bank.

Creeks

Water in rills keeps on running and running
until it flows into creeks or brooks.
Many creeks wash soil or sand from their banks
and then carry the soil or sand grains away.
Other creeks wash out pebbles and big boulders.
Water whirls the pebbles round and round,
grinding them down into grains of sand.
Water also makes boulders bump into each other,
and rubs whirling pebbles against them.
Whirling, bumping, and rubbing
wear the boulders down and make them smaller
until many of them become pebbles, too.

This creek has washed
boulders out of its banks
and is rolling them
downstream.

Rivers

Rivers are larger, longer, and deeper than creeks,
which often flow into them.
In some rivers, the water is clear and pure.
It is so pure that people can drink it,
and so clear you can see colored pebbles or boulders
that lie on the bottom.
But most rivers contain dirt, mud, and sand
which make their water look dark.
Rivers get dirt from farms, factories, and towns,
or wash sand, mud, and pebbles out of their banks.
Sometimes rivers wear their banks so much
that chunks of soil covered with grass or tall trees
break off and tumble into the water,
which soon washes them away.

This river washes mud
and sand from its banks
and carries the material
away.

46

Canyons

Streams take mud or sand or rocks from their banks
until they make valleys.
At first, valleys are narrow and not very deep,
for the streams that make them have not had time
to wear much land away.
But water keeps running and washing and wearing
until the streams make their valleys deep.
Deep, narrow valleys that have steep sides
are known as gorges or canyons.
This canyon has such steep sides
that they look almost like walls
made of solid stone.

A river has made this
narrow valley so deep
that we call it a canyon.

Old Valleys

Creeks and rivers flow year after year
until their valleys "grow up" and then become old.
"Grown-up" valleys are wider and longer than canyons.
Water has worn their sides so much
that they are not steep, like canyon walls.
When valleys become old, they change still more.
Streams wear their sides into low, gentle slopes
and make the valleys wide at the bottom.
Sometimes streams wind to and fro
as they flow through the old, wide-bottomed valleys.
Sometimes the streams spread out
till they look almost like long muddy lakes
with low, gently sloping sides.

Here is a very wide, old valley where the river spreads from side to side.

Bars

Bars are made because creeks or rivers
get more mud and sand and pebbles
than they can wash away.
The extra mud, sand, and pebbles sink, or settle.
As they settle they build up bars,
which are banks or low ridges
that often grow larger year after year.
Some rivers leave so much sand and gravel in bars
that the water has to flow between them
like a tangle of wide, shallow creeks.
Other rivers pile up bars that grow bigger and bigger
till at last they turn into islands
on which grass and trees can grow.

This river has piled
sand and gravel into low,
wide ridges called bars.

Desert Streams

Desert streams are not like the rivers or creeks
in most other parts of our country.
Desert streams are dry for months and months
in the seasons when there is no rain.
When rain does fall, the water runs into "washes,"
or it runs through narrow channels
known by the Spanish name of arroyos (ah-ROY-oze).
Water fills the arroyos from side to side;
it splashes and foams and carries off soil grains
till the banks become almost as steep as walls.
But soon all the water runs away.
Then the creeks and rivers dry up
until rain falls on the desert again.

When rain falls it
fills this desert arroyo
with a swift, muddy
stream.

Glaciers

Many high, steep mountains are covered with snow
that packs and freezes into ice.
The ice moves down slopes and turns into glaciers (GLAY-shers).
Some glaciers are short and thin and so small
that their ice soon melts away.
Other glaciers are thick and wide and long—
so long that they go for miles and miles
before sunshine melts their ice.
There are several glaciers on this mountain.
We can see how the ice cracks as it moves
down rocky slopes and over steep cliffs.
The longest glacier goes down into a valley
where the ice finally melts into water
that runs away in a stream.

Glaciers that are made
of cold, hard ice move
down the sides of this
mountain.

Glaciers get big loads of stone
as they move down the sides of mountains.
Ice pulls and pries till the stones break loose.
Then it pushes and twists and scrapes them together
till it breaks the biggest stones to pieces
or turns them into boulders.
Ice breaks small stones, too, and grinds them up
into pebbles, sand, and fine clay
that looks almost like flour.
Here are boulders and pebbles, sand and fine clay.
They were broken and ground up by a glacier
which carried them part way down a mountain,
but left them when the ice melted
into water that ran away.

Ice scraped these stones
and broke them to pieces
as it carried them
part way down a mountain.

59

While glaciers dig rocks and break them and grind them,
they also change the land.
Ice digs stones from the sides of big, sloping mountains
and turns them into steep, pointed peaks
like the one that is shown on page 36.
Glaciers change the land in valleys, too.
They scrape stones against the valley bottoms,
making them wide and deep.
They scrape the sides of valleys and make them steep—
so steep that the valleys turn into canyons
shaped like a big letter U.
Can you see the U-shape of this canyon
which was scraped and made deep by a glacier
that melted long, long ago?

A glacier that melted
long, long ago made this
canyon deep and U-shaped.

Soil

Soil is the topmost part of the land.
It is the part that lies at the surface—
the part which we often call "dirt."
Much soil is rich and crumbly and thick.
It is so thick we cannot see to the bottom
except in deep, deep ditches and holes.
It is so rich that grass, trees, and flowers
as well as many other plants
are able to grow upon it.
Farmers plow fields in the rich, thick soil
and then plant seeds which will grow into crops
that can be used or sold.

The soil that covers
these fields is rich
and very thick.

62

Soil
and
Bedrock

Some soil is neither rich, nor crumbly, nor thick;
it is poor, and stony, and thin.
Much poor soil lies on sand or beds of clay,
or on layers of coarse, loose stones.
Some poor soil lies on top of solid "bedrock"
which we see in bare hills or ridges
where the soil is too thin to cover the ground.
We can easily tell this soil from the bedrock
because the soil is not solid or hard.
Plants also grow on the patches of soil
although the solid rock is bare.

Thin, poor soil partly
covers this stony ridge
on which a boulder is
lying.

Grass

Plants do much more than grow upon soil,
for they also protect it and change it.
Here is soil that was bare except for some dust
that was ready to whirl away
when strong winds blew across it.
Now grass has begun to grow on the ground.
The grass plants spread out on the surface.
They send tangles of roots down into the soil
and hold its grains together.
Soon the grass will make a thick, soft cover.
It will keep wind from blowing soil grains away
and will turn the bare, dusty ground
into a good green pasture.

Can you see how these
grass plants are beginning
to cover the ground?

Trees

Trees may grow on the ground instead of grass,
making groves and big, thick forests.
Trees keep winds from blowing across the ground.
They keep raindrops from pattering down very hard
and do not let them wash soil away.
Leaves also fall from the trees and lie on the ground,
where they crumble to pieces, or decay.
Year after year, the leaves fall and crumble.
In time they make a soft, dark layer of soil
that soaks up raindrops and holds them.
This layer keeps the ground under forests moist
long after rain stops falling.

Dead leaves make
a soft layer of soil
that soaks up raindrops
when they fall.

People Change Land

People live on the land and change it
in many different ways.
One way is to dig mines for coal
or for the stony ores of metals such as iron.
These mines are dug with power shovels
which take out thousands of pounds of ore at one bite
and load it into trucks or trains.
Another way in which people change land
is to build cities on it.
Where city land is too high, men dig it away.
Where city land is too low, men fill the low spots
with ashes and rubbish, or with dirt and rocks
from high places that have been dug away.

Here men are
changing the land by
digging iron ore which is
then taken away in trains.

70

Plowed Fields

Farmers do not dig mines or build cities,
but they change the land.
Some farmers cut down forests of trees
and plow up the layer of dark, leafy soil
to make their fields and orchards.
Other farmers plow up prairies or plains
where grass holds soil grains together so tightly
that water and wind cannot take them away.
Then farmers disk and harrow their plowed-up soil.
They make it soft and crumbly and bare
before they sow seeds that will grow
into corn, wheat, sugar beets, cotton, soybeans,
or other useful crops.

Farmers plow fields
like this one so they can
grow their crops.

Farmers plow and disk and harrow fields
to make their crops grow well.
But if storms come before the crop plants can grow
water runs across the soft, bare soil
and washes much of it away.
Sometimes rain water runs across whole fields,
where it picks up soil grains and carries them off
but leaves lumps and stones behind.
Sometimes the water forms swift, muddy rills
that run faster and faster
as they wash more and more soil away.
Soon they make long, steep-sided rill marks
that wind across the fields.

Rain made many
long, winding rill marks
when it washed soil
from this field.

Gullies

Running water makes rill marks wider and deeper
until they turn into gullies.
Gullies may form in many different places—
in plowed fields, in barnyards, in hilly pastures,
or where men have dug steep, bare banks
beside highways and railroads.
The gullies shown on page 77 began in a hilly pasture
where too many cattle and sheep killed the grass
and trampled the ground with their hoofs.
Water washed the trampled soil grains away.
It made rill marks that turned into gullies
which grow bigger and longer and deeper
every time rain falls on the ground.

Rain water made gullies
in this pasture after
sheep and cattle
killed grass and trampled
the ground.

Wind and Dust

Wind cannot change the land very much
when fields are wet or are covered with grass.
But when dry times come, the wind is able to work.
It blows across plowed fields and bare pastures,
where it picks up grains of soil or dust,
and whirls them into the air.
When plowed fields and pastures become very dry,
the wind picks up whole clouds of dust grains
and carries them away in storms.
Dust storms are big and dark and dirty.
They make the sky look almost as dark as night
when they blow soil from dry, windy places
and carry it far away.

A big storm is taking
clouds of dust from
dry plains in the West.

Land in the West becomes very dry
when only a little snow falls in the winter
and the spring does not bring much rain.
When the wind also blows and blows and blows
it makes dust storm after dust storm
and carries away huge clouds of loose soil grains.
Many dust storms have blown over this farm
on a level part of the Great Plains.
Storms have taken away the good soil.
They have left only stones and coarse sand
which lie on bare, wind-swept fields
that seem to be as dry as deserts.

Wind has blown good soil
from this field
but has left coarse sand
and stones on the ground.

Storms carry fine dust hundreds of miles—
all the way from valleys and plains in the West
to prairies, eastern mountains, and the ocean.
But coarse dust and sand cannot go so far
because their grains are too large and heavy.
When the wind slows down, it drops them in piles.
Every wind that slows down makes the piles bigger.
Every wind that slows down makes them higher.
At last they become so big and so high
that they cover wagons and fences and sheds
with dust which the wind has brought
from plowed fields and bare, dry pastures.

Wind has piled coarse
dust and sand around
a farmer's shed and
his wagon.

Forest Fires

Lightning or people often change the land
by starting forest fires.
Some fires begin when lightning strikes trees.
Other fires start from matches or cigarettes
which people throw on the ground.
Forest fires soon become big and hot.
They roar and flame and make clouds of smoke.
They kill bushes and trees, and animals
whose homes are among the trees.
Here is a fire that is burning on a hilltop.
See how the fire flames and sends smoke into the sky.
See how the fire is killing trees
that have protected the soil
with their leaves and branches.

A fire makes flames
and clouds of smoke as it
burns the forest on
this hill.

Big forest fires burn for days and days,
or even for weeks and weeks.
But at last the fires die, or go out,
and the forest looks like this.
All the trees are burned black and are dead.
All the bushes are burned into ashes,
and so is the layer of rich, leafy soil
that used to cover the land.
Now raindrops can patter down on the ground,
for the dead trees have no leaves to stop them.
Now the rain can form swift, muddy streams
that make rill marks and then wear gullies
in the bare, burned ground.

A forest fire has
killed these trees and
burned soft, leafy soil
on the ground.

Making Land Better

Fires, dust storms, and rills damage the land
because they destroy good soil or carry it away.
But people know how to use the land
in ways that keep it from harm
or even make the soil better than it was before.
This farmer is trying to make his land better.
He is plowing clover and grass into the ground
and is mixing them with the soil.
Plowed-in plants will make the soil rich and soft.
This will help crops to grow big and strong.
It will let water soak into the ground
instead of making rill marks or gullies
that would spoil the farmer's field.

This farmer is
plowing grass and clover
into the ground to make
his soil better.

Crops
in
Strips

Here a farmer has planted his field in long strips
that run around a hillside
instead of going up and down it.
Some strips are planted with crops that cover the ground.
They keep rain water from going too fast
after it runs away from the other strips
where the ground is almost bare.
Water that runs slowly does not loosen soil grains.
It does not wash good soil away
and leave clay or rocks in the ground.
Water that runs slowly also does not make rill marks
that will some day turn into gullies
like those that are shown on page 77.

Crops planted in strips
like these keep water
from making rill marks
or gullies.

Moist Fields

In the West many farmers plow their fields
to let water soak into the ground.
The farmers do this by plowing deep, wide furrows
and by making ridges of soil between them.
When rain falls, water runs into the furrows.
When snow falls, it piles up in the furrows
and fills them with water
when the snow melts in the spring.
Soon the water soaks into the ground
where the farmers' crops can use it to grow.
Water also makes the plowed fields moist—
so moist that they have no loose dust
which strong winds could blow away.

Water that stands
in these furrows makes this
level field moist.

Growing Trees

In many places people take care of their forests
so they will not be destroyed.
Here is a forest where men keep fires from burning
and where no one cuts down all the trees.
When people need lumber, they come to this forest.
People cut down the biggest, oldest trees
but let the smaller, younger trees stand
and keep on growing year after year.
As long as men do this, the forest will live
and protect the land on which it grows.
Trees will spread their branches, so rain cannot beat down.
Trees will cover the ground with a soft, leafy layer
which will soak up raindrops so fast
that they cannot wash soil grains away.

Men have cut the
largest trees in this forest
but have left the
smaller trees to grow.

Photo Credits: p. 10, Soil Conservation Service—United States Department of Agriculture; p. 17, Allis-Chalmers Manufacturing Company; p. 25, Standard Oil Company (New Jersey); p. 51, Union Pacific Railroad Company; p. 57, the Milwaukee Road; p. 67, Soil Conservation Service—United States Department of Agriculture; p. 71, United States Steel Corporation; p. 73, Allis-Chalmers Manufacturing Company; p. 75, Soil Conservation Service—United States Department of Agriculture; p. 79, Soil Conservation Service—United States Department of Agriculture; p. 80, Soil Conservation Service—United States Department of Agriculture; p. 82, Farm Security Administration; p. 85, United States Forest Service; p. 86, United States Forest Service; p. 89, J. I. Case Company; p. 91, United States Department of Agriculture; p. 93, Soil Conservation Service—United States Department of Agriculture; p. 95, United States Forest Service.

Photographs not credited to other sources were taken by the authors.